Poetry

The Beat of the Lingo

By

Anthony N. Lalli

Anthony N. Lalli
Ants Hole Publishing
P.O. Box 277
Wallingford, CT 06492
www.antshole.com

First Print Edition   2003
ISBN, Print Edition   0-9741135-0-6
Library of Congress CN   2003093239

Foreword

For years, I mostly read American poetry and the Bible.
But eventually I began to prefer to read my own works
and it was then that I knew I was a poet. Most of the
poems are written in a free style, almost essay like, which
should make them easier readings.

However the writing of poem is far from easy, it is often
a laborious task and there are several stages. Yet, it is my
ear that tells me when a poem is finished, when it has
reached that final stage.

Perhaps it was my informal musical background that
began in early childhood that drew me to the art of
hearing music in words. It is my hope that you will hear
those same sounds that are housed in this book, *Poetry:
The Beat Of The Lingo*. But contained here is more than a
beat; there is also profound meaning, patriotism, fun, and
even bouts of spirituality. So, with practice, imagination,
and perhaps concentration, this book should be an
enjoyable addition to your personal library.

Moreover, I would like to acknowledge Emily Bedard,
of Sound Literary Services for her mechanical proof
reading and my brother Joseph J. Lalli for his input on
the graphic illustrations.

Lastly, and with pride, *Poetry: The Beat Of The Lingo*
is dedicated to the memory of my parents Antonio and
Mary.

Table of Contents

vi— The Beat of the Lingo

Chapter 1

Philosophical Tones

.

"...*God gave birth to the truth,
and made it a member of the
nobility.*"

Science

Out of a cacophony of inquisitorial pursuits, predicated on the true worth of thought, God gave birth to the truth, and made it a member of the nobility. It was born from the root of reproducibility, and it is the embodiment of trust. Yet, He then created hope, and said it must become the guardian against the origins of doubt, which would temper bouts of skepticism, and would avoid a collision between reality and frivolity.

Then, with the ferocity of His will, but not all in His image, and yet still devoid of His perfection, He made the Cosmos; hence, was created chance and conjecture, which have become the foundation of intrigue, mystery, and even rejection. As He stood in awe of these creations, He foresaw all those who would become endowed with these features to be among those with grand curiosity, and thus, in essence, He created man's future.

"Yet, it is the curves that infuse the birds' endearment to flight…"

All Aboard?

There is a depot called subtraction where man boards the subtrahend and begins a journey to an end where there is no front or back, no place to disembark. It becomes a winding passage less the bends where it subtends below passion, and transforms to flat, where some suddenly become trapped in a derailment from uncaged unpleasantries and failed commitments

Yet, it is the curves that infuse the birds' endearment to flight, and where men choose to find fault, encouragement, and the will to fight. Therefore, without round and up and down, it would be negation, that is, an elation without the excitement or man's courage for ascent; it would be a third rail, powered, positioned, and soured by discontent, in search of a tail wind.

"You would miss skipping stones across the lake, baseball games, and even fruitcake..."

Perspective

If I were to stand on the edge of the universe, what would I see? Perhaps I would see the brink. My feet and my being would be teetering on the precipice of a chemical sink, a link to where we've been and where we might go next, a history of a complex chain of events, a step beyond, a thought to respond, a point to depart. Out there, light is extinguished, rainbows relinquished, flowers and bumblebees, even if they existed, could not be distinguished.

Yet, if you were to sojourn to the total black and yearn to look back what would you see? Now observing the backside of everything, wondering and wandering into this star gaze, amazed by the morass of it all, losing earth in the forest of it all, you would feel alone. You would miss skipping stones across the lake, baseball games, and even fruitcake, but especially, you would see a glimpse of eternity.

》

But in reality, is there infinity? Is it there, and if it were, is it something we could see? As I look out my window, I really don't even know, if there are stars beyond those stars that I can see; nor do I know how a felled tree in a forest came to be prostrate, lying there, dying there, slowly decaying there, without a single soul to lament it's fate. It has been flattened, but I did not see it, so did it happen?

Thus, it is natural curiosity, to question the end, and ask, how, where, and when it will come. However, when the equation is factored and reduced to its most basic elements, when we open the envelope, and we must open it, because this is no wish upon a fairy tooth. The persuasion to break the seal must come from within, because the actuality is, and the answer is, what we have known all along, hope, trust and Truth, almost a prayer, almost a song.

"...lying there, dying there, slowly decaying there, without a single soul, to lament it's fate."

"Deep, not deadly, are time's furrows."

Dusk

Twilight, skylight, sunlight, dimmed, azure aura, halo
rimmed, speckled with sun dust gold within.

Reflections pass, introspection casts shadows upon one's
noble past. The saga courts time; time unfolds, alas.

Deep, not deadly, are time's furrows. Dusk dares us
into the darkest shadows. Forebear— a sunrise soon will
follow.

O hidden breeze behind the sun, beckoned to soothe a
sun-scorched face; succumb to find a pace for dreams, yet
to come.

"Once surrounded by an angry wind..."

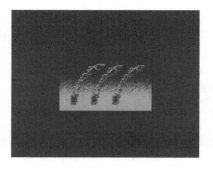

Wind Blown

When wrongly contested, men must be as strong as a stand of bended trees huddled in their own storm.

Once surrounded by an angry wind, they must find the good and not prey upon themselves in an inelastic realm.

Commence to confront and fence with the disputants in a matrix of fact emboldened on the grounds that one can rest.

Yet, if a man cannot stand in his own wind, then it would be repugnant to ask anyone to defend his stand even in jest.

"...it is the power of a free wheeling spirit that is fueling our being our creativity and proclivity for becoming more..."

Among The Daffodils

I look on the floor and I see a puddle, and my mind dawdles through the thoughts that lie just beneath my feet.

They are drowning in my sweat, surrounded by the past, and a paddle comes to mind, yet I can't find the strength, but I cannot retreat.

My ideas, your ideas, their notions, are what cause the motions, the currents, the brilliant moments, which too often have slept.

Dry land is at the edge, and I would like to hedge just a little; but I muddle, and squabble, and I do not budge, and I seem so inept.

Yet, appearances often look like dalliances among the
fields of daffodils, where the frills and the colors shield
the deliberate but delicate balance within us.

I dare out into the realm of my intellect and I detect
orbiting, orbiting among the abstruse and obtuse,
floating and tumbling, are the ingenious and ingenuous.

Yet, an element of spent hope is not a settlement for
less, because the difference in a single valence is the
imminent emergence of a puissant isotope poised to
soar.

However, it is the power of a freewheeling spirit that
is fueling our being, our creativity and proclivity
for becoming more, forgetting we may only fumble
forward, as never before.

"...it is the power of a free wheeling spirit that is fueling our being our creativity and proclivity for becoming more..."

"Distinguish between truth and inept perception."

Contemplation

Cease fraternizing with your own frivolous
frailties and look onward to your particular
capacity, created and ignited by the courageous that
can do, rather than dutifully dwell on some hollow
malady, though you are miffed, you are still woefully
wallowing in full view.

Walk and debate life's innumerous contradictions.
Distinguish between truth and inept perception. The
trees will endear and endow such a stranger and dress
you in armor to fight off extinction; you, predaceous,
engaged, enraged, and endangered.

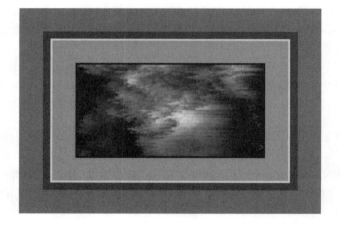

Chapter 2

Light Hearted Vibes

"...it would create such a ferocious wake branches would brake, and I would awake..."

Autumn

It was a time when the trees were fire red,
and the sun was full overhead, without the
scorch, then suddenly, monstrous bumblebees
began to buzz just off the front porch.

I slunk down in my chair, and I tried not to
bolt, making them believe I was not there,
but out of the balmy atmosphere blared a
tumultuous jolt that electrified the air.

Then the diving, the tumbling, the zigging,
the zagging— it would create such a ferocious
wake, branches would break, and I would
awake, only to find piles and piles of leaves to
rake.

"Tolerate the indomitable dogs and hounds disinclined to abate."

Opportunity

Cliffs, briers, bogs, mires, and arbors abound. Tolerate
the indomitable dogs and hounds disinclined to abate.
Yet, patiently harbored, poised in the tree, is the cat—
besieged, besmirched, beguiled, pondering a fretful fate,
aversely perched above where a befuddled dog just sat.

Dedicated to two family cats, Alice and Ruby Begonia

"...it's a part of the dark, more of a beam, a glow, a spent spark."

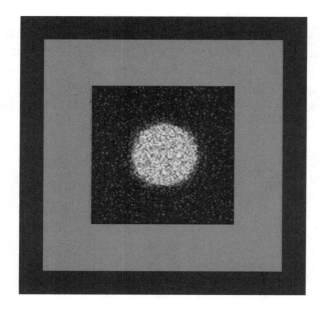

Moonlings

When was the last time, you looked at the moon?
Viewed its gray texture, its ancient mixture?

When you took a look, did you find the sun?
It is there. Stare. It won't blind anyone.

When you think of light, you think of life.
But is the texture dead? Is it just a sky fixture instead?

It is a solitaire, a suspended host, extended out there in
the universe, a part of the first, a speck of the cosmos.

Rarely do you see it by day. It's a part of the dark, more
of a beam, a glow, a spent spark.

Surrounded by a spectacle of glisten and brilliance, you listen for the crackle of fire, only to find the silence to inspire.

Look far out into the night. Then shout, to see if they can hear, but don't fear that they might.

Maybe all that black does have a crack, a beginning, an end, and they too carry their lunch in a sack, to share with a friend.

Why would a cow jump so high, or a witch zoom by on broom?
Surely not to say hi to a gray dark lump, but could they want to say hi to those on the moon?

Why would a cow jump so high, or a witch zoom bye on broom?

"...so dreadfully cantankerous, aggravating and tactless, so vial, yet, they have a certain appeal to us."

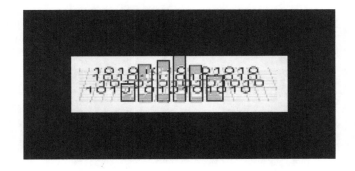

Satirical Computer Speak

These congenial electronic creatures are so resilient, so kindheartedly pedantic, cerebral and elegant, so stylish, and— they have certain gentility towards us.

Such plodding plastic pleasures are so superficial, so dreadfully cantankerous, aggravating and tactless, so vile, yet— they have a certain appeal to us.

These seductive synthetic saviors are so brilliant, so splendidly analytic, agile and diligent, so meticulous, and— they have a certain civility towards us.

Such temporal therapeutic treasures are so artificial, so exceedingly egregious, infuriating and endless, so hostile, yet— they have a certain feel for us.

Chapter 3

Patriotic Steps

"...lying among the stench of battle, I am fouled in the shadow of the enemy's grapple."

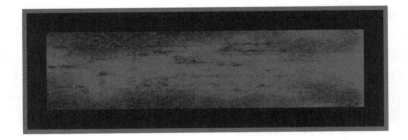

The Twelfth Night

Digging a ditch can sometimes be a stately act, notably when it is a statement of duty and freedom, yet every soldier's hitch forebodes to bear that load upon his back, for liberty in all seasons.

So, in this trench, lying among the stench of battle, I am fouled in the shadow of the enemy's grapple. Only honor can be my battle song, so clang the bell and clamor for the wrongs to be settled.

But next, I am hit, and it is every bit as hurtful as hurt can be, especially for my first Gethsemane. Yet, tantamount to my whole, is that I am about to have an Epiphany; if not for me, so for my soul.

*"Summoned to duty once again,
called from cold chiseled granite... "*

.

Duty Eternally

Pungent poignant odors of battle surround
and saddle our souls. Silent is the nectar
of introspection that once was around, as a
scent of aberration in a ranting town.

Tearfully and tenderly, we remember them
in this tranquil air, somewhere about,
nestled in the shouts of cheer, a solace for
those courageous hearts.

Summoned to duty once again, called from
cold chiseled granite, etch after etch after
etch, called to comfort their friends, who
lament and never forget.

"...is the heart, which directs the direction of thought, the founder of the start."

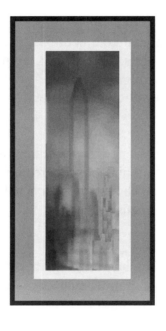

The Arsenal

To catapult your dreams beyond the pull of the earth is
never simple.

Whiz by streams of debris; witness the birth of black
holes that extend from sea to shining sea.

But peculiar to people in flight, as stark as dark and light,
are precious principles that peer just over yonder.

Although appropriate apprehensions duly sends a signal
and draws cannon fire, yet, peculiar to principle, one
stands unfettered, foils fear, steers the rudder.

Fire one! Heart pounds. Fire two! Implode; expose bare
bone. Fire three! Aye, aye, storm the eye, but never with
a drone.

Reload the breach, gather your breath, and breathe to
the depths of your deepest thoughts; Lord we beseech . .
.

»

Far from perception but dear to creation is the soul, is the
heart, which directs the direction of thought, the founder
of the start.

Hold on to a dream; hold on to something so
basic, so serene, so intrinsically simple, hold on to your
principles.

When finally you become percipient to the
triumph at hand, then forearmed, you become a recipient
of the gallant, the stalwart, and the steadfast stand.

Forever more laced with power, feel the
turbulence, the exuberance, from the ethereal flight, the
arsenal's might.

Hold on to a dream; hold on to something so basic, so serene, so intrinsically simple,...

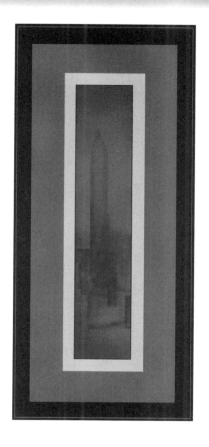

...some will discover barrels of dreams analogous to...

Only In America

Dreams that are hollow usually are carved
out of fluff and pillowy stuff, so without
much substance they are plunged into state of
emptiness and their gases can engulf us.

Yet, deep in any crevasse of the brain's
wrinkles, some will discover barrels of dreams
analogous to cucumbers and pickles, that is,
today you are one thing, but tomorrow you can
be something else.

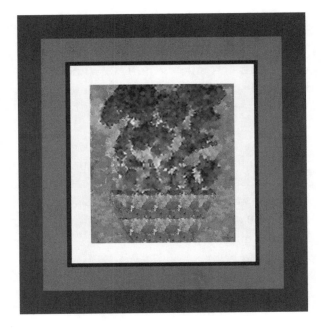

Chapter 4

Nature and Seasonal Rhythms

"Then frogs would croak, prod and poke, to hop, would be out of the question."

Fog

Descend, down, on every creature conceived from the
Creator's kingdom.
Then it would be morning; it would be dawn; it would be
sunrise without the sun.
For clouds would be cloaked overhead and would choke
every shadow to oblivion.

Descend, down, without a sound, on every city, village,
and town.
Then birds would beckon for signs, but senses would blur
in search of a beacon.
For sparkling brooks would babble and boast of foregone
radiant reflections.

Descend, down, cover the earth, and hover over the lakes
and ground.
Then frogs would croak, prod, and poke— to hop, would
be out of the question.
For owls' suspended stance would lose their intrepid
trance and introspection.

Descend, down, fill every crack and crevasse and
perpetuate every man's frown.
Then crawlers would creep, but cats would no longer leap
with perfection.
For spooked deer would shake their fear of their
foreboding perpetual predations.

Descend, down, suspend aloft, and overlay the land,
conspicuity ne'er the champion.
Then meadows' greens would gray, as if nights and days
were in clever collusion.
For darkened crystalline blue skies would petition the
sun, and struggle to reawaken.

"Then crawlers would creep, but cats would no longer leap, with perfection."

" *...enmeshed, in marsh soaked bending rickety trees, whistling whirling oak leaves...*"

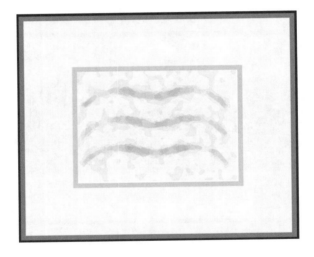

Winter in Charleston

It is a blustery day; the breeze has bloated the clothes on the line and painted the embers red in the chill. Inlanders ruefully remember the stately hills, but then hurled aloft and sent adrift into the frosty air, are the fliers.

Climbing higher, they cut into the wind's swoops and swells, making loops and circles, where kaa and keeow resound over the town. Among sounds of distant bells, far from the safeguard of the ground and shipyard, the fly birds soar.

A virtuoso of echoes invisibly immersed in a visual splendor enmeshed, in marsh–soaked, bending, rickety trees, whistling, whirling oak leaves, turbulent seas crashing and splashing the rocks, and boats bulling the waves and bucking the docks.

"...spring begins hunting for the sun and a duet of songbirds begin dueling again;"

Perennial

In the early morning when the birds have just stopped snoring, Spring begins hunting for the sun and a duet of songbirds begins dueling again; then buds, swaddled in dew drops, start peaking through dollops of shadows spun from sprigs of grass in the meadows, as shades of green caress them whilst canopied by the yawn of the wild blossom.

"It is the still, and the chatter of the leaves."

Indian Summer

It is not shrill, and it is not clatter.
It is between a colloquy, and a clamor.
    It is the wind on the trees.
    It is the sound of a breeze.
It is the still, and the chatter of the leaves.

It is not a trill, and it is not a flutter.
It is between an oratory, and a mutter.
    It is the wind on the trees.
    It is the sound of a breeze.
It is the still, and the chatter of the freeze.

Chapter 5

Cultural Chants

"...a lust among weeds, where the law indeed has blown."

The Trial

Where there otherwise would be natural jumbling,
instead it becomes juggling, and here lies an intersection,
where some begin stumbling, into contrivance. Lured
by the seduction of leverage, and the fear of losing, men
have abandoned randomness, by their own choosing, and
thus, it is where prejudice and outcomes are born.

Nonetheless, the treachery of this trial, was not in
the stylish triumph of the defense, nor was bias the
only vicious victor to be found abhorrent. It was the
grandstanding that tried one's sense of rationality, and
hearts were aching to adjust the ballasts, but in practice,
it was forsaken, in absence of malice.

Yet, the most evident split was at the outer limits of dusk
and dawn. At this juncture in time, came the indictment
of the judicature's divine structure, where there was
a disavowing of excellence, a lost flower we should
bemoan, and the bowing to insolence, a lust among
weeds, where the law indeed has blown.

"Thunderous thoughts torment nations totally."

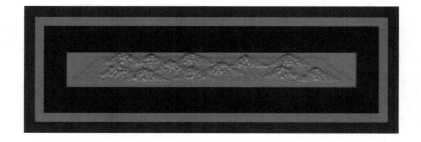

Peace On Earth

Scurrilous, scathing words, sounds reveille.
Thunderous thoughts torment nations totally.
Penchant for peace foredoomed, with ponderosity.
Rapprochement, bridges rancorous blunders boldly.

"...and brands all of us with a touch of seething menace, in a maligned niche, just a notch beneath humanity..."

The Cynic

Charged with opinion and challenged by beauty, with
dominion over the sepulcher of skepticism, he totes the
scepter of incredulity and dotes upon the uncourtly and
envenomed suspicions in men, all for naught, except
what lurks in hopes to unearth some demonic plot,
cloaked in truth and forged from utter puffery.

A face with foreboding scowls, he stands watch,
with exploding howls, at the first sign of a scorched
possibility, and brands all of us with a touch of seething
menace, in a maligned niche just a notch beneath
humanity, as he beckons the race to become hardened,
and frowns on man's taste for pardon's amnesty.

As the wretch of the lampoon, and the forbearer of mistrust, he deems himself the interpreter of truth, the slayer of dreams, and the sentinel of fallibility and disgust. Thus, a sleuth in a bastion of opinion, where vision is but a dragon's drink to him, he dips his pen in an indelible ink well bound for stardom in hell.

Often the inelegant equivoque of elocution, and blackguard of a perverse tomorrow, his forehead is furrowed with surprise, as he plows through a field of impending demise with focus on some unending sorrow, thus betrothed to the ill-disposed, where conquest is a joined battle of minds, in half–truths and lies.

What would startle and stagger most men, he is the host of disparagement from them, and will growl and glower, even from the scent of the most delicate flower, or sees the marvel as he cowardly ponders and somberly unravels them, eerily spewing impudence and luring legions into the purulence of his undoing.

Clad in a foul molten acerbity, as though mad from a scrupled gate, never to find kind kinship from a soft supple endearment, so he worships tender mercies, finding hardships and unfounded conspiracies, with nothing to appreciate but tales spun at the expense of men. So behold him but a forlorn scornful sentiment.

"...the edge of doom is not always among the squalid, but rather, it is just a solid quid pro quo argument away..."

Dodge City

Moral purpose is popularized by the notion that good is better than evil, and that a smattering of God is not so smothering when you consider that the devil is a blithering fool coveting your soul. Yet, the edge of doom is not always among the squalid, but is rather just a solid quid pro quo argument away; a tit for tat will do, with remorse seldom ever creeping so close. Why aren't there any more horses still tied to hitching posts?

*"But a fool's reciprocity,
is the repugnant retort…"*

The Chicken or the Egg

When fencing with bullies, one tactic is to finesse, cajole, and, perchance, stall, only to be mauled by such flimsy and flawed antics. Indeed, reason has lost its reverence in such a case, where facts face off with futility and struggle among defiance and hostility. Thereby buttonholed, men's bellies sometimes become bloated with an ambivalence, which blocks the heart from a natural eloquence of thought that ought not to be locked in the soul.

Yet, to be vanquished by words, is to be cherished by no man, especially, since one cannot simply vanish from view. But a fool's reciprocity, is the repugnant retort; purportedly, rogue members of a bitter tongue, not far from the ghetto, and contrary to acceptable vocabulary, hence words that have abandoned the mind's afflicted constabulary, often the breath of bravado, and heretofore, are depicted as deplorable, in defense of one's ego.

»

Where, but in the jowls of their mind are such words that lumber and linger, lying in wait among expletives that mingling about, in obscenity, profanity, and even blasphemy? Wherefore, but belligerence can stir such a frustration inside, and detonate a powder keg of emotion, fomenting from the dregs and bowels of perhaps the contemptible, that too often laps into the patently unpalatable, hopefully retractable, but inescapably, an inedible egg.

"Wherefore, but belligerence can stir such a frustration inside,…"

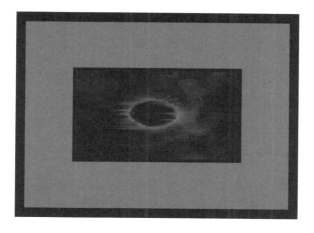

"Rather than cultivate the sodality of healing and the universality of kin..."

Group Theory

The founding of contempt will never cradle the chance to be exempt from those ideas, that when done, enhance the worst in men. To sustain the identity of ancestry, some conceived of the group, where incubation nurtures the future realization of enmity, and the birth of the perpetual loop. Generations become lost forever because their convictions backfire, generating fractures that inflame, and sons and daughters with misdirection, which create disdain, again and again.

While it is intellectually sound to gather around and express clever notions of conquest, men become lesser, and eventually weak. Yet, it is the conceptual man's attempt to dupe, and that they are the mothers of civility, disregarding the others who remain reticent to speak. Rather than cultivate the sodality of healing and the universality of kin, they perpetuate the unraveling of man's common origin, and the essence of this hurt, is a fear that lurks within, from when they began, again and again.

"...it would be difficult to meet a bird or butterfly, profiled as ever being a mild malcontent..."

City Parks

The sun looms, beyond the pale, in the midst of a blue sky, and we ask why? Walk down any big city street and it would be difficult to meet a bird or butterfly, profiled as ever being a mild malcontent, or consumed as a vassal, or bedazzled by brewing events.

So city lungs are filled with flight and flowers, all meant to temper the mind, designed to regenerate, and to find a way to recapture the rapture of the atmosphere. Yet, there is something unclear, cruel, so amiss, and perhaps perceived as a duel beyond the architecture.

It is this: frequented thoughts summoned in the park are interrupted and expelled, by the hustle and flow of the city's muscle and clout, all concocted to disrupt a shoot—out, just north of hell, all in the name of law and order, to quell the fury of a bedraggled and surly desperado.

"So to wit, his lips script a lot of dribble, but not so subtle blandishment..."

Insincerity

Wheedle she, wheedle dumb, and so says the beat of the
enchanter's drum, as he meanders among the beautiful
women. Wander to, wander from, meander rampant
among the old and young, and so says the philanderer.

Assuredly, some cossets, incognizant of the absurdity,
are cuddled, coddled, and sold by the lure of the
delusion. Thus, they are bewitched and cajoled in an
idiom, which applauds deception but shrouds the flaws
and indignity.

When chivalry crumbles, and tumbles to none, then the
hellion becomes numb to deviltry. So, to wit, his lips
script a lot of dribble, but not so subtle blandishment,
with a little, but not more than a trickle, of sincere
sentiment.

Among such frailties, with a paltry touch of truth, this
is not a dim–lit torch. With an allegiance to lust, he can
scorch the heart, inflict injury to trust, and be derelict to
the best of what is lovely and precious.

"A great thirst for truth hopefully can be seen in a word."

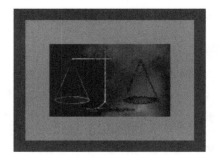

In a Word

A great burst of breath hopefully can be heard.
A great thirst for truth hopefully can be seen in a word.
A great jury for justice someday the docket will be required.
A great understanding for underlings should never go expired.
A great pulse for pain hopefully can be seen in a word
A great call for calm hopefully can be heard.

A great burst of "besought" hopefully can be heard.
A great thirst for thought hopefully can be seen in a word.
A great shame for shunning someday the rocket will be sired.
A great anger for anguish should never grow tired.
A great disgust for despair hopefully can be seen in a word.
A great hope for healing hopefully can be heard.

"Therefore, it was the sun that perhaps, created trouble."

The Onset of Our Differences

Earth basically began as rock and dust, and the rest simply seemed to be there without purpose. Then came the streams and the oceans, but never a dream; it started out, by what appeared to be hopeless. Yet, hitherto, time was measured in billions, and all in preparation for an explosion of breath. Now, I have seen life, just the way it may have looked at its origin, and I still remember what it was like, and how I thought Van Leeuwenhoek might have felt, peering through his microscope at his little animalcules from Holland. But as I pondered among the beams of reflected light, all I could see were similarities, a cluttered collection of clones, and life without a brain or backbone. Yet, if I were to call out someone's name, everyone would look, so too, at the onset, this is how it was, until a scorching sun cooked everyone, and created conflict. Par nobile fractrum was about to fracture exactness. Shapes would lose their uniformity by attacks from newly formed amorphic genes, and what was once the top, it would now be called bottom. For the first time, the emergence of designer beings would abound. It was the dawn of disjunction and multiformity, the concept of resemblance would be turned upside down.

»

Heretofore, things appeared black and white; now it all looked so muddled. It is hard to believe today, that life probably began in a puddle. But when evaporation began to set in, and for the first time there was a shortage, then everyone began to compete for the same bowl of porridge. Where there was once a grand dinner, now it was the scrappings and cheap wine, and it would only be a matter of time, where either they would adapt, or be lapped up by the sun— so born was struggle. Therefore, it was the sun that, perhaps, created trouble. Now, instead of everyone wanting the same thing, there would be those who would switch from drinking wine to drinking gin, and hence there would be diversity. Thus, not all ate porridge, and not all drank the same beverage. It was the beginning of difference, and thus the early workings of the law of averages. So as change began to emerge, each of those that stood out, said they were unique, and rather than converge around similarity, they discovered divergence, and it led to perhaps peculiarities, which eventually leaked, into what we regard today as individuality.

"... then everyone began to compete for the same bowl of porridge."

"Black possesses no color."

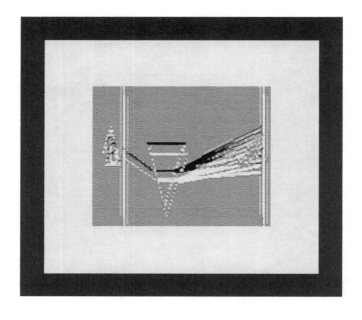

Color

White possesses all the colors
Yet, Whites do not consider
themselves colored people.
Black possesses no color.
Yet, Black people are called colored.
Why is that?

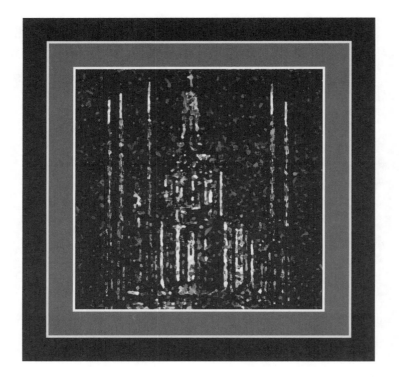

Chapter 6

Inward and Soulful Movements

"Take mirth, it is the mother of caprice, yet it cannot be dug from the earth, nor lugged around in a suitcase."

The Object of Love

An object is something that can be measured. It may, or may not just sit there, but then again, it could be mobile. On the other hand, it may, or may not give us pleasure, but then again, it could have that potential. So an object, such as a man, is in a state of being, or is in a state of becoming, or, we could just say, man has the potentiality of a thing, or perhaps, he is what he might have been.

But what if, an object is dismissed as a mere speck, or say, something exists, but it can not be weighed nor boiled, yet, is said to carry weight, such as love, dignity, or the state of being loyal? Take mirth: it is the mother of caprice, yet it cannot be dug from the earth, nor lugged around in a suitcase. Behold, the measure of a man, is not bound to all the gold and lace, but abounds, in the object of love's solace.

"...hence flowed the poet's first words, and thus composed was a form of music."

A Prelude to the Poet

I believe that in the beginning, the intellect of man was awakened by the Soul, and the first thing that he understood, was the beauty of the bird songs that he had heard.

Then God said unto him, this is what is called good, and man eloquently concurred. Hence flowed the poet's first words, and thus composed was a form of music.

Now, both were songs, absent a written note. While once undreamt, one was from a feathered creature, the other, a primal overture as man was smitten with hope.

"...they were thrown into holes with less than gregarious cats."

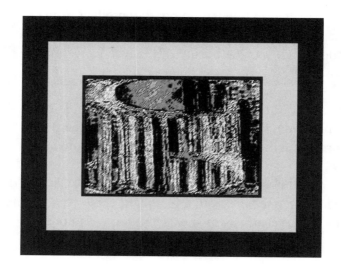

Collaboration

Christians collaborated with God and
they were thrown into holes with less
than gregarious cats. Some thought they
were simply being criticized for their
nefarious plots, while others surmised
that some sought to silence their Souls.

> *"...a sea where rocks, fog, and lighthouses grow, and where only seasoned captains, might fare a good blow."*

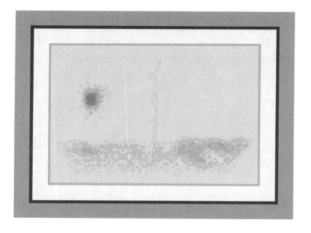

Sea Ghosts In Hell

Frogs, crocodiles, and typically landlocked creatures would never dare to venture out to the sea; a sea of whitecaps that lap and lick the wind, a sea that has chapped and cracked many a pirate's crass skin; a sea where rocks, fog, and lighthouses grow, and where only seasoned captains might fare a good blow. Yet, fathoms down, strewn in the canyons' ground, are hulls, masts, and echoes of cannon blasts.

Gulls avow, that they watched it go down; now overhead, they eye skulls beneath, some with daggers still clenched in their teeth. Bird cries pierce the sky's emptiness, which harkens witness to that Armageddon. Oh mourn not, not for these forsaken souls beckoned by scavengers' calls. Lest a flier forget, all these unsung barbaric outcasts are mired among the sea grass, and avenged by fire from the cannonballs' flash.

"Stoically, I journeyed in the dark, marked by the sound of music."

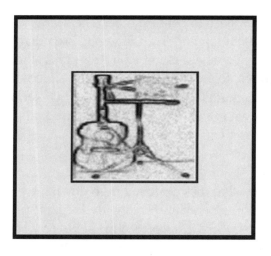

Connected

When I was in the belly, it was then that I began to bolster the idea of eternal motherhood; it was then, that I unequivocally and unexpectedly understood.

The blood ran through my veins and hers to sustain a fragile existence; it mustered the strength in my callow fiber, for sustenance, that embodied life's essence.

The pound of my heart and hers stirred, first in pure harmony and then symphonically. Stoically, I journeyed in the dark, marked by the sound of music.

Parts became the whole, the very soul of one, simple in being, like God to the Trinity, as the breath of the sea is to salinity, for without each other, neither could be.

I reject the notion that they ever disconnect, and I expect they never do. Conception is the start of a match, a medley, a miraculous cohesion of the two, for eternity.

The graphic art, was done by the author.

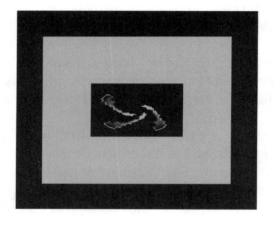

"...He then created hope, and said, it must become the guardian against the origins of doubt..."

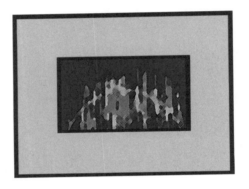

Index

Index

" I *believe that in the beginning, the intellect of man was awakened by the Soul.*"

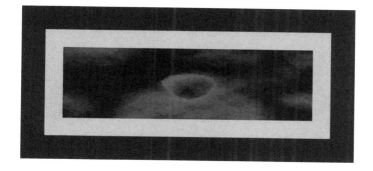